IOWA

BY
LUCAS HUNT

Lucas Hunt

NEW YORK
THANE & PROSE
2016

"A cowboy ain't easy to love and he's harder to hold,
And it means more to him to give you a song than silver or gold."

—*Mammas Don't Let Your Babies Grow Up to be Cowboys,
lyrics by Patsy and Ed Bruce*

For my Grandma, Mom and Sister

CONTENTS

WILD ANIMALS

The waking have one world in common.
Sleepers meanwhile turn aside,
each into a darkness of their own.

     –Heraclitus

I asked my father if he
was afraid to walk at night
alone. "There's nothing there
but your imagination."
What about wild animals?
"They're more afraid of you
than you of them, but if
one comes close, get away
in case they're sick and bite."

THE BEGINNING

I stand in a field and listen to wind
    become water on my skin,
no words, just hawks in the sky
    and wasps in the swing set.

The corncrib swells with rock hard
    cobs of multicolored grain,
a bull snake coils around my leg
    I step from its boot-like grip.

A field is an ocean of green leaves
    the wind waves on my skin.

CORNFIELD

Emerald waves applaud midsummer's
undulant hills, honeyed kernels,
amber tasseled stalks inert,
wind-wisped leaves stir earth's aroma,
slow circling suspensions of time transpose
a dust blown cloud, adagios of air,
granular infinitudes above
a gravel road, long grassy ditch lined
with barbed wire fence that goes nowhere.

Barbed wire fences
overgrown with weeds.

I change another flat tire.
A snake slides in the dusty ditch.

All that's lost may be regained
in the passage of clouds.

A faraway train sighs
and sunlit grains of corn

lay scattered on the road.
Redwing blackbirds eat.

Wind whistles
through the pines.

Mud puddles in a lane.
A water tower tops the hill.

Fields roll under power lines
and harvest the sky.

DIXON REVISITED

Here tall corn pivots in a thunderstorm
children and adults scream,
an empty kitchen
holds coffee cups and cobwebs strung
corner, warning siren, to corner.
Figure eights of lightning
dance on the floor.
No one is here that was not before.
Thunder cracks a rib
and reports in criminal quiet.
That spirit which is immortal in us
cannot be killed.
Take small-town walks,
bike rides down streets of yesterday
with back alley dogs, fireflies
rise from earth in a reverse rain of light.

DOWNTOWN MORNING

Cigarette smoke cools a cloud
drifts out the window.

Downtown is busy we delay
work to make love.

Out of a physical world
spirits are born—some visible.

    It is daylight
    we deeply
    desire
    to sleep in.

Just one more kiss
a mirror reflects the sun
the city is background music.

AS THE CROW

To get from me to you I walk out of town
on graded gravel road, rocks thick
no tire tracks then abandon it.
The number one empty can of beer
in ditches is Busch Light.
At a gate marked *No Trespassing*
Danger Sewage Lagoons
warm in the sun—
(Dad, the plumber, says shit bakes off)
a flock of geese does not care
what's in the pond.
I cross a fence
and hack weeds with Grandpa's
walking stick, hug the steep muddy bank
of a creek that ain't clean,
thorns to the calf.
A fallen tree becomes a balance beam
over the creek, the other side
a soybean field—
soft green leaves gently gyrate,
legs hurdle rows
up hill to a grassy patch where it happens;
the perfect spot for conception,
vantage of creek and field,
miles of countryside
open open open.

➤⟶

One day we will picnic
with bottles of red, white and water
the whole day,
bread, pickles, cheese and terrain,
have our way on a blanket
with the lavish, eternal, pregnant earth.

GIVE YOUR HEART

I've not seen the sun set enough
  to know the meaning of change.
Long winged hawks fly above
  and cast their shadows down.
"Give your heart to the hawks,"
  Jeffers said they are worth it.

HAWKS

They take the air like words in blue display,
planes of rain that pass with outspread wings
and ride round the sky in sure, slow turns
to hunt hypnotic, float and dive—
birds witness wider fields,
their eyes survey a storm and pass
through light that changes everything in space.

UNDER THE WALNUT TREE

Once I sat on a ledge
and swung my feet into the distance.
Valley wind funneled
through the beans
caressing leaves
gathering momentum
washed over years
and crashed into concrete.
Still the rail vibrates in my hand.

Today the local auctioneer empties
two by fours and metal rods
from the pole shed,
a black squirrel spooks
and ants crawl crack to crack.
The old tree stands ready to give back.

There's a hole in the sky.
Winds meet and permeate like fingers
clasp in coalition, to become one
is uncontrollable—one day you will feel it.

WALKING

With dogs on a gravel road
dust from the passing
truck plumes
into a cloud over
the soy and corn fields.

FROM THE EARTH   (for J.C.V.)

When I was a girl earth was
older than apple trees
a small stream
wove through fields
brown from rain
our house
the grassy hill
cattle grazed all summer
a frog pond
in full moonlight.
I was a girl in the country
dreaming ocean
and storm,
fat drops slapped leaves
under the death-toned sky.

I challenge twisters take my
life none dare the fury
prophetic shapes
in my bed
wild tongued

➤⟶

bolts shoot through me
throwing stars
nothing undoes
the knot or penetrates
darkness monsters
my cave,
each day ruin would suffice.

A seed burrows in the sore
no reason to speak
thus unspoken
so write about fate
the wildest.
I might stand
in a field
water voice about
to cascade
the taste of sex
a vortex
sun on skin waves
splashing rocks
perhaps over and over again.

BUENA VISTA ROAD

On a gravel rock road
I dream of our times long ago.

The gold luster of summer
reminds me life will not last forever.

Tall grass and wild roses
paint the ditch in pink and green,
manure on the field
is the smell of money here.

I delight in visions of cornfields,
long leaves wave, silk tassels
in a sea of shadows.

At the lagoon, I turn back,
blow a grateful kiss to the wind
and think no more of you.

DOLLAR AN HOUR

It pays to listen to pigs scream
a few times a week,
to shovel shit and blood
into a rank pit.

Over time, crap turns to dust.
It stings eyes and fills
lungs with black phlegm—
best suffer in silence.

You learn to grunt
bare the weight
of tired bones
the stench will not wash off.

THE STRUGGLE

Irons of nostalgia ground me, copious plains,
I plow endless earth for air, leap in lakes
    for relief from humidity—
The struggle is hard to throw off.

Heartland of sorrow,
Who dies for the corn and wheat,
Who pilots tractors through swollen fields?

Part of the past is dead, part is pregnant
    and yet to be discovered.
Who are we to abandon yesterday?

I will not return to see silhouettes
    of trees cool against the sky,
    a pink and blue sunset
Behind farmhouse, silo and shed.

Shadows sweep the field, stretch the sky
And obscure backgrounds of one
    thousand dusty towns, turn
    window screens gold
And bring rest—wild forgetful
Bushels of laughter under the stars,
Loud in isolation, far from a highway,
    free to fly in the night.

HIRED HAND

Dirt roads wind through fields
of cattle, crop and weed.
Farmers lean on bales of hay
rest their backs and legs.

Meat on a grill, beer in a barn
whoever works the field
shares in this reward.
Tomorrow comes early.

A TIRE BURNING

The sky is restless
clouds merge and break apart.

Fire is a song of red
and orange and blue
flames dancing
from underground,
eyes and ear listen
but must not be consumed.

When our neighbor throws
a tire on the inferno
black smoke rises
an ever-widening plume.

Burning rubber
is a temporary landmark
over antebellum barn,
buried train track, fence crows
and dirt piled by a bridge.

It's a pissed off snake
until the wind sweeps smoke
away and sunlight returns.

WAPSIPINICON RIVER

Wind bends grass by the brown river.
Crickets chirp and fish splash
a bird call, dog bark
black tree leaves.
Bugs buzz
a crow caws twice.
Cotton clouds
are gas gods,
no flowers or music
but wind.
I apply mud
from the banks
to my skin
and become rich
all over again.
Silent empty branches
butterflies play
in the sky, airplane over trees
the beat of a drum.
A twig snaps the surface
ripples and glimmers, someone sings.

WHATEVER HAPPENS IS TRUE

Rain that wets the eye is true.
Light that breaks the sky unearths
words that sound like wind—
tomorrow, heaven, soon.

Days multiply and change
as the dew evaporates.
Night separates and the dark
that blinds us is also true.

THE LEGION

Evening wind blows right
on a muddy country back road
I ride on
my father's motorcycle
gripping a trash bag
one-quarter full
of empty pop and beer cans,
counting telephone poles.

Our Saturday ritual
pick up cans from ditches
and return them
to The American Legion
for ice-cold
Dr. Pepper and Old Milwaukee.
Cigarette smoke drifts
over liquor bottles.

I'm too short to shoot pool
or the shit with truckers
or farmers so sit
on a stool to watch the Cubs
and listen to Old Hank
on the jukebox.

LEAVING THE FARM

Hunger drives a boy
to break from walking beans,
sweat soaks his clothes
there's nothing else to do.

The wind calls in a voice
that grows loud each summer.

Lighting brands the sky
and prophecies new work,
rain washes barnyard
shit off his skin.

Ready like a deer
he runs from field to forest.

THE TRUCKER

Bright lights and signs to the clouds,
metal dinosaurs pause to refuel,
engines shake pavement
and growl.

The night is loud
for tired eyes and haggard faces
who need a job driving cross-country,
who can stand the strain of driving
away from family.

I've seen the sunset a summer evening,
fallen under spells of gray and gold,
watched soft explosions of purple
and white disappear,
I know the slow silent feeling of home
fades in the rearview.

But what the hell,
why stay in places that gather dust?

I shoot to and from that orange ball,
confront the enemy time
gunning a long flat broken stripe
and know it all belongs.

And here is my snake of artful transport,
goodly image recreated, congress,
dear dark power drawn to mirror
mud and salt, thin strands of mortal
flesh that twisting question air;
king of man forsworn upon a stately
bough to answer—were all as involved
other work would not get done.

MUD CREEK

Bugs swarm steep grassy banks
and weeds to the trees
brown water
slides through fleshy mud,
soft hill, cow pasture
by an abandoned rock quarry
where kids jump
from cliffs
to swim in summer,
through farms
rich with animal manure
past a firehouse
out of town.
They call it Walnut Creek
but what about
the leaches, tipped canoes
and trash thrown
in it for years?
It'll always be Mud Creek to us.

REACTION

To see the face
as it rises
from a pillow
eyelids part
to light
and pursue
the kiss
before she
returns to sleep.

TO A SPARROW

Trill perfections of flesh, annunciatory
bird, levitation passing lively song
above an umber field, plowed rows of dirt
infuse the annual melody,
morning hovers on wing and lights
a lucid brow, swift clouds of dust convene
in tillage of fresh-blown air, you
escape the blast and land
under bent stalks of newborn corn,
gone for an instant, reappear
to raise accelerations of chipped tune,
imperfect singer, fitful salvation,
graze the tips of leaves and dart along
overgrown ditches tall grass pivots
in wild circulations to nest,
share with young a little fodder found
among wild pink roses
and pendulums of dusty weeds galore
then hasten over a gravel road
to maneuver a sea of soybean plants,
still visible yet flitting
in a breeze faster than I can foretell—

➤—→

I wait, you fly, my land your sky
what happens above falls
in burning fields, a solitary sun
has set upon emerald hills, transforms
the world into a vivid dream
as you pass in figments of time,
average bird divine, reach the horizon,
deep sobbing violet body of air,
note the base vacancy and disappear.

TO YOU

Suspended hair feathers
wave like leaves;
nature's hand
applauds in the trees.

DAVENPORT

A big barge floats under high clouds
men fish by a theatre
the train howls
smoke in factory power lines
gulls circle
boats docked on shore.

Water flows east to west
down the levee
a fish by a white buoy
skirts a mossy log.

Cars span a bridge
anchored in the riverbed
a bell bangs
in a tower beyond the lock and dam.

BIX BEIDERBECKE

Drown Mississippi ballad for tomorrow,
for floods of brassy blues to celebrate
the too-blue cavity above us all,
vortex of sorrow and madness and joy.

Music allays, a horn says more
to posterity than thousands who heave
through humid streets in late July, too paced
runs fame at those who can survive.

Surrendered serenade, grim coronets
blasted the note inside you then exhaled
the living strain, sporadic ecstasy
of playing what's not been heard before.

WHEATLAND CAR WASH

Because our town has less than others
no gas station grocery store
(once upon a time
train station
hotel tavern cobbler plumber)
we drive to Wheatland
which has two bars plus the assisted
living facility Grandma likes.

Rusty and dusty on blacktop pavement
American flags in yards
train trestles piled by the tracks
country on the radio
deer sausage
chills in the bed of our Chevrolet.

Stop sign, fire hydrant, phone pole
a train whistle
red lights rocket and bells ring
boxcar after boxcar
passes a downtown vacant lot.

The pressure washer blasts
our truck as clean as it will get.
Dad takes a pinch
from a can of chew and rolls
down a dripping window to spit—
fresh manure on the field, smell of home.

BEDROOM WINDOW

Tonight the shooting
stars are showers.
I am blind
to feel the earth
for holes
to crawl in.
Airplanes
come from clouds.
Love breaks
through my window.

ON DANDELIONS

Apart from undulations of green grass
a warm wind lifts light chariots off dome
and gives a weedy flower to the lawn,
diffusive, lemon spokes of summer sun
reflect on fluffy parachutes released,
small flying feathers
seed the air with panoplies of hair
that drift and land in universal yards,
penetrate the earth with long taproots,
tender leaves, raise their stems
and multiply fine florets—
soft, aromatic beds of yellow heads
transmit a solar energy, surprise
an eye with possibility:
wine, salad, honey, medicine and tea
compose the herb, its milky stalk
a bitter fuse of bent diversity
that bows in wind, ghost engines blow
through webs of space, broadcast parasol
like offspring and circulate
airborne puffs that send
their stuff across a span of blades,
propel the tiny grain to fly on fate,
transport numb dust

$\rightarrow$

born to sow tomorrow
or perish the instant, capitulate,
fall and blast off again,
rotten recovery empowers all
the seeds that ride on wings and sail
to different pasture to sew their gold
in monotonous lime carpets.

STRINGS

Wind scatters the dust
and is gone. Shadows converge.
There is a way to move,
there are infinite ways to see
what happens this time.

Light enters a window
and cascades to the floor.

Air rushes in as it opens
to the noise outside.
Streets and sidewalks
are empty yet footsteps echo.
A faint harmony strums.

GRANT WOOD

Who unrolled the countryside and painted
panoramic fields, furrowed rows of dirt,
golden shocks of corn and hay?

Trees balloon over barnyard, emerald hills
prostrate to unsown pastures of air,
pale saurian shapes above
archipelagos of gas, swift infantries
shade grassy waves of prairie—
limestone silo, serpentine creek, windmill.

But always first the farmer and his life,
mother, sister, father, family
portraiture supreme. Who happened away
from everything to champion home?

WALCOTT STREET

Everywhere you and nowhere you
among dilapidated houses,
driving Main Street
people still care.
I see your eyes in faces
at the ball park, truck stop
bar and vineyard.
There are moments
when dreams come true
and breathing changes
they are nameless.
But I know it's river
and moonlight
or sugar, flour, water and eggs
and hot peppers
and cake itself.
Traffic shifts down to go up hill.
Fields billow with nautical flourish
under overlord clouds.
Who can quit life
without taking one last look
down the alley?
The lawn is ready to mow again,
aunts and uncles are ready
for the kind of house
cleaning no one wants to do
except auctioneers, who solve problems.

SOON

I felt you drift away
now I know you are here—
house on the hill
a semi-truck
works its way up
sunlit patio
diamond in the fields
we sit on bleachers
everyone related
or not from around
here the creek
post office phone company
back alley bike rides
open windows
each morning
sit on the front porch
a bowl of breakfast.

CICADAS

In evening comes the insect siren from
fortresses of pine, shrill unisonic
hum that pulses limb, threads rhythm
round dense layered bark in labyrinthine coils
to the core of spiral-formed cone
dropped to the ground,
where nymphs burrow, grow and ascend
tree trunks, split their scaly skin
and molt into adulthood—
swarms of unseen song, a weedy string
of palpitating sexual play,
sharp sound permeates the atmosphere
loud gusts sway imbalanced branches
jade needles gyrate
a maddened tune, odd whispering
of sky entombed echoes, shadows commit
chill suicide on nature's floor,
grass hisses, wild vines climb barbed wire,
reedy barrage under wood canopy
the noise incessantly ravishes,
what lies inside a shell, what hellishness
abounds the nervous mating organ
and mirrors existence like
no other, no locust of dumb mind
with fibrous drums expounding, cymbals crash,

>—>

no silence surrounds nor distance
undoes this animal bleating;
quack on strident bug, hidden sounder
between the sappy boughs of magnate trees
I get your hysterical message.

DISTRACTED BY MESSAGES

As a crow laughs
corn on the cob is better
nothing on it
and pie-eyed summer
shouts to whisper
do not bother
perched on head
cloud drizzle
has a light
you walked without
what happens
we seldom realize.

CALLING

Lake borne urges come to fruition
ripe watermelon juice down
both cheeks, pink rinds
smile from the sink a friend
calls late at night to talk about love.

It's July, high season, nearly August
birds mad for seed and squirrels
nutty from heat, dogs lie
in the shade, the sun does what it
wants to skin the soul aches.

Red bird, black bird, blue bird
on the lawn watered twice a day,
beer, bourbon and nuts
replaced like last weekend
with this—take a bus
or train or hitch a ride to get away.

Tuesday feels like Saturday
because the heat, hammocks call,
bicycles await feet in driveways,
rain is cool your voice
a relief, one thousand miles
do not matter, the happiness is ours.

MAQUOKETA CAVES

We hold our breaths and enter underwater,
    flip on flashlights and crawl
On hands and knees through rocky tubes
    no map to the labyrinth.

Accidental entombment in a tight place
    comes to mind, we go headfirst
On our bellies to an underground palace,
    slide like worms of inward truth
Few will witness, spelunkers are insane.

So much lies below the globe's thin surface,
    ancient people packed the earth
With plants, seeds, jewelry, tools, bone—
    priceless artifacts tell a story.

We grab the gnarled roots of trees,
    kick at fern and spider web
To see farther in the sky than before,
    laugh at stars because caves
Are deadly closets and life is worth
More now than it was before having risked it.

THUNDERSTORM

The low and humid music summer sounds
from clouds drops cool beads on
thin boards and glassy pools.

Unseen insects play the weedy melody,
hours of heat finally release,
sink into verdant hills, flowery fields,
acres of vegetable and grain.

A vein of lightning sears the sky
and fades into the fixed design of things.

LOVERLESS SUMMER
FOR BEN AND MONICA

I'm stranded in a good way, without you,
in a small town far from the sea
the stars are visible.
A lawnmower, owl, country breeze
stirs a curtain it's the first summer
which feels like the last.
Once I promised it wouldn't end.
How many times can you fall in love?
This is Iowa: no cell coverage, taco pizza,
a wedding reception, a bar
down the hill from Grandma's house
college up the road.
My aunt and uncle arrive in their Mustang,
doors open to project
horse images on the driveway.
They have a cooler full of sweet corn.
How do you do it, not that
but remain in love?
I ponder miracles to escape
a wrong relationship, birdsong, frogs
and crickets sing in chorus here at night.

THE APARTMENT

It is like walking
into a room
or body
not a place
to live.
A room is life
and there
is time.
A room
is there for you
to visit and leave.

FOR ANNA

Marry me my Mississippi muse
in a maze of flowing streams,
a rush of constant currents,
a flood of momentous ease.

Below a waxing summer moon
crowds gather on levee lawn
to hear jazz performed
or else attend a ball game.

Either way the fireworks open
multiple flowery explosions,
a train hoots by the park—
something impresses everyone.

There's a festively lit bridge,
boats bathe in the night,
orange auras on the water—
everything impresses someone.

And the river responds,
"love does not cancel out love
but blood bleeds into blood,
it all becomes one, a dream."

TORNADO

It's a normal day the wind
Mouths nothing in our ears but routine,
      cattle chew the grass
Of rural silence on plush hills, people drive
        home from work
In nearby towns, or farther off,
A city candidates visit to get the vote.
Cell phone towers poke the eyes of riders
And guide wires outline concentric pyramids.
Riverboat casinos bring gamblers,
Losers can ban themselves from boarding
      an unlucky boat
Or end up getting kicked off drunk.

    (The sky goes dark)
It rains, pours, thunderstorms
Eerie ambiance covers the earth,
Violence shakes trees, haze grins on hills
A dark plate eclipses, dips down in
      a menacing manner,
Drops a fiendish finger from the clouds
And strikes and sucks and detonates all things.

There goes a volatile tunnel of destruction
That mows trailer, car, dog, barn, fence
        aluminum, concrete,
Whips debris and hail on hood and roof,
Hits someone on the head and blood
        soaks their face,
They run for cover, traumatized by nature.
Some sit on porches and sip refreshments
        to a radio forecast,
Phone family members or tell strangers
        what they possess,
Why they worry, how flight is futile,
        go to basements
Or leave their chairs to look outside
        a nursing home window,
Pray or freak out or make love unaware.

Some do not leave their barstools,
They watch the television report and grin.

    A few fear the danger let loose
        yet welcome disaster,
    Shake a fist at demonic wind,
        yell epithets on high,
    Taunt the twister with names,
        cry havoc, court death.

Gone to wreck elsewhere,
It's not like negative judgment comes or bad
        luck or a witch's curse,
We know the world is wild too late.

THE END

Something shakes leaves
from trees
bent like blades
of grass.
Ashy clouds
freeze
the evening sky.
Summer ends
in dusty whirlwinds.
The country spins
into a dream.
It's dark—the sky
undresses
and lays down to sleep.

LEAF, MOTH, FISH

The leaf falls like a feather from a tree,
spins and hits the stream's surface,
waves gently break a reflection,
boulders dash down hills.

The moth bobs up and down
like a pigeon pecks at scattered seed,
huge cotton clouds drift
like kites above blue mountains.

The fish comes up for air like a sprout
in spring, I leap from rock to rock,
sunlight frays to shadow
and fades like footfall on a frozen pond.

THE HUNTER

The hunter knows what's about to happen,
After work he sharpens arrow blades
    with stone, shaves his arm,
After work he's hungry and ready,
After work he bends his bow,
The string is tight and hard to pull.

The path to the timber is dirt and dust,
    the drive is short,
The hike through the field is quiet.

The hunter bows his head before nature,
He walks into the solitude of trees
Fortunate to breathe.

Unlike other animals
He smells nothing, instincts lapse, imitates
    to kill (man is poor if not for
    brains, brute intuition,
And camouflage—he's just a predator).
The hunter enters the wilderness
    by becoming it again,
Responsible for food, he starves or learns
To match his will to another.

Hidden by leaves and branches in shadow,
One with the woods, watching aloft,
The hunter cradles his bow.

He pictures prey to the stage,
Fingers tension with stealthy hands,
Lifts and draws with gentle arms and holds
    life within his sights.

Then aims and releases an arrow to the deer,
The sharp shaft pierces its heart,
Feather and split tip enter fur, tear flesh,
    the deer falls to the grass,
Its spirit loose, neck arched, head pivoting
Around for one last look, collapse.

The hunter touches the body of the deer
And feels nothing but his own pulse.

DAY LILY

Once concealed in night
a rural flower opens,
light deftly lances
the orange petal gift.

MY FATHER

I owe it to the man
Who made me out of nothing to grow under the sun,
Who baptized me in rustic weather, planted food
      to eat and drilled wells to drink,
Told stories to rhyme and inspire.

Who knows in depth
About foundations, plumbing, thermodynamics,
About electricity, lumber and mechanics,
      the concrete of family,
Love of neighbors, relatives and dear friends,
The wind whistles through the pines.

About how the days
End soon in autumn and sometimes melancholy sets,
How green hillsides turn yellow and orange
      before the harvest,
Grasshoppers fiddle, bullfrogs croak,
About those diamonds as big as horse turds.

IOWA CITY

Too many dawns did wrestle darkness long
to penetrate an ashy moon and break
that spell, funeral atmosphere,
phantom in the night—
where sages lose like fools and age
is a myth of timeless time,
where beauty runs the street and torrefies
the feet of passerby, not a bad town
but one to leave for sure or else sojourn
there forever bewildered in a crowd.

THE POISONED WELL

People came from miles around
To a metal pipe in the ground,
Small mouth of an artisan spring
Flowing into a shallow stream,
To fill gallon jugs with water.

Not everyone thought it wise
To sip straight from the well,
Most said there was no harm
But some decided to test it,
'We want to be sure,' they said.

Who could suspect the fields,
The very fertile, very fertilized
Fields had saturated the earth
With cancerous chemical salts,
Now few will dare to drink at all.

ODYSSEY

The fall of 1995 I went to Iowa City
to go to university there,
everything excited, ped mall
to city limit train tracks.
Dorms were dull
but a bunch of guys
from Chicago roamed the halls
quoting Kerouac, Ginsberg
plastic cups at keggers
and suburban tales.
Got the lay of the land from walking,
ate chili sauce on white rice,
cigarettes, a haircut,
pawned bass guitar and amplifier
for a new bike.
A Maltese woman
stopped me on the street
and said keep walking like that.
Road trip to Mexico South Dakota
California Arizona
tent in a park
by the hospital helicopter pad
rode Greyhound
hitch hiked along the coast
fresh cardboard under the overpass.

HARVEST

Corn leaves tan and dry in dusty air
tassels shake before the blade
tractors travel dirt lanes
men dig and heave
machines harvest
men use their muscles
then eat and sleep
I dream of purple clouds
that brush the sky with blood
until it's time to go back to work.

ELEGY

In Iowa City sorrow you know
so well, rain from clouds
puddles under bridge.

Walking at night I call ululation,
shadows in wet streets fugue
and rapture, life returns
and lightning is a penumbra.

Where are coasts with rocky shores,
wind from the ocean, sunlight
and smiles on a beach?

In separate places now
we are free to remember our bond,
many seasons have passed
since we raged, it feels too long.

THE DIVING ROCK

A sleeping bag, six pack and cigarettes
with King She aka queen of the hippies
driving out of town
gas station where I was cashier
an overgrown lane
tree shadows connect fallen leaves
branches on the ground
we shuffle down.
Blue sky, dark water, reggae
and a motorboat—
light on the reservoir, ring of rocks
and trees and meadow
turkey vultures fly from cliffs
we imagine death
accepts us back into the universe.
Fear comes
before the nerve
to dive twenty-five to the lake.
The climb up is tough
then share a victory beer or smoke
"who's ready to jump again?"

MOST WALKS

There was a contest among college
students for most walks
home in the rain.
Poets won—
their hearts
pitchers ready to pour
and be refilled
but suicide
takes it's toll on everyone.
Rain is cathartic.
You can only imagine it
so many times before it happens.

MY GRANDFATHER

He communes with mountains,
   hikes along their peaks,
enshrined in Appalachia,
   forever told to speak.

THE FARMER

Who gave more and received less
    then died before his time
If it's possible, who lost his life,
    family, land and legacy,
Whose reward for work was work,
To grow food and raise animals
    for the world to eat,
Who but the farmer, a father,
    son, husband, brother, friend?

If somehow still alive
Would he do it all again?

Some say they know how hard
    the work is to survive,
How hard it is to get through days,
How hard it is to pass the night
    alone and know the end.

Water his grave with tears,
    thunder out a litany,
Tear down churches,
    burn graveyard grass
And scream about injustice.

Forgive him he did not know
Time has no purpose, God no promise,
Life is endless for those who love,
    even forgotten it continues
In the acts of unsuspecting people,
In the physical celebrations of nature,
In the ongoing debate for improvement,
In the spiritual transformation at death,
In the eternal movement of energy
    and existence of ghosts.

Change to another set of clothes,
They contain the cologne of barn
    and field and garage,
Are dirty and hang heavy on your limbs.

That decrepit costume is no longer useful
Now the suit of an afterlife or nothing
Heaven, oblivion, reincarnation
Infinite possibility.

Yet who can be accurate, who knows
    anything for certain,
Who can say what comes next?

AUTUMN

September burns an ephemeral flame,
strikes and recoils in blue,
roses abandon verdant terraces
and wild dandelions die, a city too.

THE FUNERAL

On a Sunday in the country
neighbors gather to mourn their child.

Brown dogs with tired eyes lay
before a weathered house.

Locusts sound the fall
vines tangle in wire fences.

Cars and trucks line a half circle
driveway and park along the road.

Voices carry out the kitchen
to friends and relatives in the yard.

The mother says a prayer
in front of her congregation.

The sidewalk is split, black and yellow
flowers litter the dry lawn.

Swallows over the field, sunset casts
a wagon shadow on barn doors.

On a Sunday in the country
neighbors gather to mourn their child.

FLOWERS FROM THE DEAD

They do not breathe them anymore
so each September I reclaim
the best a graveyard has to offer,
a colorful arrangement.

The dead do not protest too much,
flowers die at first frost,
why let them decay when
my neighbors enjoy fresh displays?

SCATTER THE ASHES

Over sodden fields, cattle indented,
that ankle-twisting terrain,
plant and tree and river,
fertile ground where the floods
deposit rich material.

A flat-bottom boat fishes in pasture
once run by rodents,
to row across the countryside
with our dog Hope
as co-pilot, solitude's a treasure.

When fields dry they leave behind
frog ponds and turtles,
swimming hole, winter ice rink,
grass prairie—as for ash
this is where the dust will settle best.

REDFIELD

I wander around town your death
twists a big wood spoon
in my stomach
strangers
take me to their table—
I am one
of them voices leave
the kitchen
what remains
in a room without you?
As you walk to your mother
a train whistle sounds too loud here.

OCTOBER ON A BENCH

In a low murmur wind-
blown water ripples
in small waves,
rolls like cars
downhill.
Dead grass hushes
an airplane jet
railroad tracks pound,
a scream
pierces leafless trees
by the window.
Runners pass
on gray sidewalks,
a robin
flies away.
The wind lifts
a crisp leaf,
flips and smashes it
on a rock
by the river
it drowns in dark blue.

OF WINDY TIDES

Windy tides break through morning fields,
overthrow tan leaves on grassy shores
and wash the fog of night away—
drown empty tree boughs
in fresh blown air, energetic flights,
before harsh gusts of winter arrest it all.

DUCKS

Lonely fowl oblivious to cold
with oily quills to keep them warm.

There's something about bright
feathered ducks floating on a river.

They paddle to land and waddle,
unable to run, fly low—splash.

Little orange webbed-feet motor
them unaware of being ducks.

They search for bread and mate
as gulls scream and geese honk.

Blackbirds chirp from the trees,
ducks frantically preen then stare,

Dip their bills in water, gyrate,
taste the air, wag their tails serene.

They quack and leave white clouds
of remote offering to fish below.

WINTER

Brutal phantasmagoria of snow and ice, another cold
        prosecution, morning drudgery
Wind stings you awake and breath is a cloud.

Cruel atmosphere, narcosis of white whispers
        murder, murder, murder
Will get you, polarity blast your bones,
This is the season to suffer.

The planet was once a barren clod of nothingness
        until by slow degrees
Of solar eminence, sunlight warmed a galaxy
        of indifferent matter,
Fire fell to earth, god in the flame.

Now a blizzard blocks the sun, apocalyptic flurries
        sweep the arches with frost,
Expose candle hearts to glacier logic, hoary hills
        wipe out evergreens,
Comas of cold lead to numbness.

I command the nearest house to hibernate there,
        blankets, meat, hallucinate
Fresh blood on the snow, anarchy of frostbite
        then succumb to sleep,
White crystals do not hurt anymore.

Snow on a field, wind in the trees,
Cataracts of fluffy stuff surf the slip in time
        and nuance in between,
A scream, icicles snap from a frozen gutter,
The premeditation and seizure, blood on the snow.

DRIFTING

White waves drift over
roads and crest like desert dunes
forbidding passage.

ONLY SNOW

Falls yet raises an eye
to heaven above
passing
power line
and dendrite limb—
only frozen
water crystals
hold the illusion
of something
that is really nothing.

WHERE THE TREE FALLS

Neither side of the fence is our land
Yet we gather the wood for fuel,
So perform a favor for the rancher,
Whose horse and cattle would get
Out in spring, and farmer, whose crop
Would crush if the still-standing
Half of the old tree finally collapsed.

We cross a snowy pasture together
To reach the fallen-half, cut it up
And load big logs on the truck,
Then take down the standing half,
Timber, it crashes in a field
On the other side of the fence,
Broken limbs evidence of our work.

Though it was intended for the tree
To fall in the opposite field, not
Drop in thorny brush or snap
The wire fence, we still had
To drive the long way around
A pathless plain of uneven earth,
No small task for one father and son.

>——→

Yet we did what we set out to do,
Gathered up kindling and returned
Home to chop the pile of wood,
To burn piece by piece in a stove
And heat our house all winter long,
Together we unloaded the booty
And split the slivered logs with axes.

TIMBER

In winter noon invades a hollow tree
with pendant light, snow glows, wind nails
a whiff of fresh cut oak, that's the stuff.

TRACTOR REPAIR

When massive steel blades
thunder to break
ice from frozen rivers
of pavement
birds scan the wreckage
of tire tracks
for grain.
Our work arrested
disking field
planting, harvesting—
earth is a womb
that turns
seed to food.
Winter ground
gets back what's taken
by crops
a buried treasure
under our feet at all times.

INVOCATION

There's an inevitable, final frost then ample sunshine
And frolics on the lawn lead to weekend drives,
Brown water in the ditch, wet country,
        scent of thawing earth.

Out from the house,
Stuffy air, empty bottles, dusty books,
Free from stews and spoons, isolation's spell,
Time to rake the earth and plant new grain, a fume
        to levitate to life again.

To burn the dust of rooms, open windows
        to the soothing breeze,
Unclog a fountain full of pebble, stick and seed,
Time to resurrect the spider web.

I crave the source of life under the sun,
That sole object of sight that blinds us to behold,
        catapults through space,
That celestial pendulum of raw energy, light carnival,
Yet will sing about it another time.

We burned it down, went through rooms
one by one, gas gushed from the metal mouth of a can
soaking dry wood floors. Part of the volunteer
fire department came with a truck,
drank from a free keg of beer
in case (the pines). First the smoke
then a forked tongue of flame licked the window
frame inside out and the house exhaled with a boom.
A pile of empty maple syrup bottles
in the yard, they called him The Pancake King—
(we dig a hole and bury them)
Old Herman kept his goats indoors.
His brother Ott lived up the hill and dumped
trash in the river. Before the horses went
away dad drove us to see
the land, parked a rusted green truck
at the gate and asked, "can you imagine living here?"

Acknowledgements:

N. Thane Boulton, Ben Cawiezell, Sarah Weis Denton,
Emily Dorcas Dixon, Jesse Elliott, Jacqueline Farrara, Matthew Frazier,
Sarah Gerard, Jack W.C. Hagstrom, William Hathaway, Mary Hevy,
Mark Humphrey & Larry Rundy, Thomas Hunt, Sarah Jones,
Richard Kendrick, August Kleinzahler, Gina and Peter Koper,
Cael, Cole and Chad McCarthy, Jeffrey Nolte, Lukas Ortiz,
Murat Oztaskin, Mary & Philip Spitzer, Jessica Sylvester, Michael Tyrell,
and Joanna C. Valente.

Thank you dearly to Madeleine, Christina Daigneault & Simon Van Booy.

Lucas Hunt is a celebrated American poet who was born and
raised in rural Iowa. His work has been published in *The New York
Times,* and has received *The John Steinbeck Award* for poetry.
He lives in New York City.

CPSIA information can be obtained
at www.ICGtesting.com
Printed in the USA
BVOW11s1414220517
484736BV00001B/3/P